I0170758

The Northern Line

by Dominic Stevenson

Winter Goose Publishing

Winter Goose Publishing
2701 Del Paso Road, 130-92
Sacramento, CA 95835

www.wintergoosepublishing.com
Contact Information: info@wintergoosepublishing.com

The Northern Line

COPYRIGHT © 2015 by Dominic Stevenson

First Edition, March 2015

Cover Art by Ladd Woodland
Typeset by Odyssey Books

ISBN: 978-1-941058-28-2

Published in the United States of America

Mein schönstes Gedicht?
Ich schrieb es nicht.
Aus tiefsten Tiefen stieg es.
Ich schwieg es.

—Mascha Kaléko (1907–1975)

Contents

*To those who help make the world a better place
by loving enough to do positive things*

*To my mum for taking my books away when I
misbehaved, teaching me their value—and for
telling me that you can find a comfy chair to sit,
rather than just sit on a comfy chair*

*To my dad for shouting at me, louder than at the rest,
from the touch line*

I

The Sullied Towns of England

No one talks about us.

Once boys and girls,
we're now men and women
in the sullied towns of England.

No one visits us.

Even if they did,
they'd scratch through the surface
of towns that get worse
each passing year.

No one walks these streets.

This land
is given away for tuppence
to private enterprise.

Some believed it'd get better,
that investment would replace intolerance
and flood the streets.
But the rest knew
growth was a myth.

Those that could leave,
left.

Those who couldn't,
stayed.

Those who left
now look at the moon
from a rooftop in a new town.

Bastardised,
simplified versions
of those now gone from sight
are reproduced by those who stayed.

The rest of us
watch the dirt roads
as they trudge
never looking back.

Queen's Speech

We speak Monarchy
and look like money puppets.

Centuries of betrayal
through forced subjugation.

No abdication.

Move no more,
says the Colonialist.

Spend some more,
says the Capitalist.

Complain no more,
says the Privileged.

Embodied beneath the crown,
the subjective face
of objective truth
is withered and worn.

To turn against them
is treachery.

Terror makes for complicity
and a working mass.

Oh dresser of my notes,
face of my coins,
be gone.

We need no more heirs.

Hardened by Hungry Nights Does Not Make a Scrounger

He queues for hours
so his children
won't go to bed hungry.

Once a hero of the community,
he stares at the table of food.

He thrusts Yorkshire tea bags
and canned stew into his rucksack,
naked at our whimsy.
There's not enough food,
and he knows this.

He mutters
a *thank you*
cloaked in shame.

He must go home
unarmed with dinner.

He'll have to come back
next week,
hardened
by hungry nights.

Front Line Love

Politicians create fear.

They send boys on missions
made for men.

They don't give enough training.
There is never enough training.

Boys.
One,
by one they fall.

Show them how to shake a hand
before they fire a bullet.

Show them how to line up,
how to love again.

In the Sunset

Hijacked pride
of red cross
on white.

The flag,
blanket that warms loins of tyranny,
and false royal prophets,
that enslave soldiers.
They pillage
remains of families
for their life time
to waste on destruction.

No One Can Tell You
How to Walk

Take your liberties
fought by heroes past.

Take them,
burn them to cinders
and spread them over the ground.
Sweep them up
into dust bags,

drink them up
and become strong.

Muscles are taut
and tense.

Hearts pound,
thump.

Sweat drips
from a battered brow.

Carry those who need help.

Make sure
there is no such thing as neglect
or peril.

Only the echo
of strength.

Be the Love in the World

The might of a fist
can batter you down,
or become hope.

Be a beacon,
shine through
and show the way
to those who need you most.

Be a leader.

Forgive
and you dissolve fear.

Forget
and you perpetuate the agony of history.

Be a teacher.

Don't give power to a suit
who can't walk
the common street.

Be the voice that says *no*
and offers an alternative.

Protect the vulnerable
and give your life
to end tyranny.

Smile,
and the world changes.

Word Watching

If you speak a cruel word
destroy it
with a kind lullaby.

Frivolity
makes for a gentle mind.

Hide your voice
for yourself.

Do not let blackened governments
use your words
for their goals.

Stand guard with sentiment.

Make your statement
with a grin
and stand true.

Your words matter.

Brent's Bells Toll for Freedom

My soft palm holds
an appointment card.

Ten a.m.,
I'm born again.

Mother tongue
is left at the door.

The trek
from one place
to another
fraught with problems
of its own,
has seen earth,
sea, and strangers
whip past windows
and miss destiny.

Here,
it rains over the brick,
the rain drenches stone.

Oh sweet London drizzle,
how I've longed for you.

With Her Majesty's blessing,
free passage awaits
from home to abroad
to home again.

Crush Our Benefits

Two up
and two down.

Two middle aged
and two young.

Eight legs
and eight arms.

Four minds,

white.

Breaks for the married,
the middle.

No help
elsewhere.

Sustainable living
for *the Suit*,
who said
enough is enough
to the poor,
the disabled,
the ones hardened by time.

Carry Those

You carry those
that hide from life,
whose dignity is stripped,
and queue for pittance.

It's not easy
to drag onwards
with what your parents taught you,
what your teachers forced you to learn:
liberty and positivity.

After the struggles
of the year before,
you make sounds
with a new voice
given by forbearers.

Now you owe them:
pay the tax,
reap the benefits,

it's what heroes died for,
what politicians argued for.

An expectation of infinite support?
You're apathetic.

Now you're called to fight,
only to keep what you have,
even with so little left.

Call on Me to Purge Your Pain

Tell me I can stay
on the grass
near the driveway.

Allow me
to sit next to you,
thigh to thigh.

Don't lie,
or change the truth
to suit you.

The rain mixes
with our tears,

the umbrella torn.

I turn away.

You hide from me.

We are shamed,
maybe forgotten.

Jeans Burn in the Flames

Think of the children
as they burned in the flames
of that Bangladeshi factory
where your jeans were made.

When you try them on
think of their families
fined their daily dollar
for non-delivery of goods.

When you look in the mirror
sideways,
think of a week's wage.
Gone.

Take your change
from the cashier,
open your wallet,
stuff in pennies and notes,
and check the receipt: 15.99.

Winter sales
mask the pain
of the dead.

Stamp Your Feet

Question corruption
when it defies
the ideals of
men and women
who've sacrificed
so you can tweet.

Stamp your feet.

Stamp,
stamp.

Walk on their backs
until they listen
to our demands.
Commands.

Don't stand and watch
the birth
of a bleak future.

Stamp your feet.

Stamp,
stamp,

even if we might lose,
let's stamp together.

Lady Liberty Disguised

You show no evidence
you stand for liberty.

A woman gets twenty years
when she defends herself
against domestic violence.

Universal healthcare
is *no-no*,
so people starve,
fall ill
and die,

a wrong that can't be undone.

Guns are hidden
in jackets,
held on to by child killers,
but tampons in courthouses
are of major concern.

That's *OK*.

A scrap of paper
signed over two centuries gone
says you can do
what you want.

One Day Catastrophe
Will Ally You

You make paupers
fit for crossbones.

Blind to youthful masses,
you toy with integrity
over profitable vice.

A beggar is a rich man
practicing a poor profession.

You wasted each coin on excess,
gamble to move decimal points
across a light parade.

You should mourn
and allow sorrow in.

When you turn brave
and take the place
on the stand,
more will come,
placard in hand
and bring others.

Placa de George Orwell
(Eric Arthur Blair)

I zoom in
on her lipstick-stained cigarette.

I follow her legs down
a black skirt
to a stiletto.

She turns the corner
at Calle de Arai.

Back the same way.
I follow.

I stare at her long
wispy hair.

Her keys dangle from a chain
hooked at her hip.

My fingers play
with the camera
and a pack of gum.

East Berlin Chic

Berlin's ideology crushed
and separated people.

A past gone.
Pushed out,
stolen.

A tortured young
burned to ashes,
no longer walk.

Where they stood,
I now stand,
my back against
the hallowed,
graffiti-covered stone.

Turning Down the Chance at Redemption for a Country in Turmoil

Mascha Kaléko returned many decades ago to stand on a stage, but she turned down an award, circumventing the country's will to wipe a slate clean. Her ghost still stands and stares at a nation's outstretched hand. She doesn't offer forgiveness. She is a reminder in ink that some things can't be so easily redeemed for trophies.

Journey to the Kingdom

Departure gate 14
is void of heaven.

My name is printed
in black block letters
on the back of my boarding pass.

I tuck my passport
into my jacket,
safe passage.

Her Royal Highness' scrawl
is etched on the inside.
She grants me access
to places some won't go.

At the check-in desk
they scan my papers,
laser my eyes with theirs.
My fingers tap the counter.

I make it to the flight deck,
ascend to my seat,
onwards
through the clouds,
the skies.

Paradise is at 36,000 feet.

Down there,
others wait
outside the terminal.

II

Intimacy on the Underground

Parts of his body fell
on my lap:
a thigh,
a hip,
a forearm,
a breast.

I move away from him,
but he expands,
grows on me,
into me.

We are one now.

I have his thigh,
his chest,
our heads
one head.

We read the book,
turn the pages
with our fat fingers.

Tube Strangers

No other city
has lights like you.

Down tracks,
a flash of yellow
making scratches on
branded windows
dance.

Tunnels connect,
and I make eyes
with a stranger.

Vampire Commuters

They suck the blood
from your neck
if you decide to lean
near the edge.

Stand behind the yellow line.

Let the dead disembark
before you board.

Eager elbows provoke
a snip of skin,
and an eternity

on the Northern Line.

Paris Gives You a Table

We closed our eyes
and held hands.

Towers
made out of paper.

Boats,
toys that float in a bath.

Love,
padlocks on the bridge
waiting to be bought, etched,
unlocked then secured.

You love the view
from a thousand steps up.

We Drank Beer at Midnight

Under the icon,
we treaded the pathway
with tourists.

The delight we took
in unknown paths.

Drunk,
we spilled beer
on cobblestones.

Our hands were occupied
by metallic canisters,
our lungs lit up
with smoke,
eyes twinkling
in the on the hour
light parade.

Salad in the City of Love

We dipped toasted bread
in vinegar and olive oil,
and I kissed the fortress
of your smile.

The stars,
were like tiny olives,
that lit the path.

Our forks pushed
into the green leaves,
poked at the feta.

I kissed you again,
ate you up,

a mouthful of home.

Love Swimming

Sun creeps in
and spreads over our arms.

We ignore Mother Nature's alarm,
cuddle and giggle,
and flaunt our love.

Shadows cast over tents and trees.

Back under the blanket,
we talk of the lake,
of jumping in
feet first.

The Heart (All We Ever Wanted)

I surrendered
my good nature
to fear.

I close my eyes,
the sun goes down
around me
and casts my shadow
on the tarmac
outside our house.

Gentle,
your voice in my ear,
your hand in my hand.

Heart touching
we called it.

We give it another name,
love.

We Built a Fortress Out of Pillows

Sordid in style,
we hid
from those who wanted
to breach our walls.

We lay,
made out on the couch,
not so broken,
not so battered,
resting on the cushions
of our eyes.

She Is a Love Pioneer

She trail blazes the city
of my heart,

slides down ventricles
with no shame,
bears her naked flesh
and false promises
of a long stay,
before she takes
a lone dive
into the atrium.

She resides in a small hotel
off the side of my ribcage,
and buys lunch along
my arteries
where meat is served raw
with no side salad.

Now she's the size of a fist
and makes me cough,
clench at my chest,
aware of her presence
with every heave.

Silent Talk

We wrap our legs
in a halo of skin,
no socks
to protect us
from the cold.

We are the fiery
centre of the world,
the place with fingers
and tongues.

Hold Me Hostage If I Want Run

Is this it?

Take the initiative
and tell me.

You are in the heart,
in the space where the beats
bounce off the cage.

If you just try,
we might not die here.

We Are the Beating Heart of Us

We contemplate
which came first:
the navel or the sunset?

No selfishness.

Every day
we share our pain,
and make room
for another kiss,

how it frees us
from words
that hurt.

We Imagined Flowers

One night we danced
in the kitchen,
and then tip-toed
down the hall
for more wine.

On the way,
we imagined flowers
growing from the floor.

We held on to each other,
and danced across the flowered carpet
and onto the couch,
where we lay naked,

our skins touching the edge
of the cushion,
our hands,
open palmed,
against the heads of tulips.

Night Raging

We shot the moon,
slashed it,
set it on fire,
burned it to the ground,
danced around it.

We howled like a siren
and were caught
in the downwind.

Those who heard us, wept
as we ripped
the night in half.

How to Switch the Light On/ Darkness Off

No one knows
what flicks the light
on and off
in the sky.

Maybe force of will
or treatment sought?

My unknown quantity of self
is shrouded in shame
for what I can't control.

III

Drunk Talk

The fire pit turned to embers
and illuminated
the last of his guests.

The ones around the fire
sat and waited
to hear him talk of his past
shared with people that mattered.

Instead he wept,
but the crowd demanded
he speak.

Loneliness broke out
of him like a slipped yolk.

He put his hand
over the pit
and he sparked a smile.

Exit Here Death

Unable to change his past,
he parted from the flesh.

The train,
burst like a fallen star,
fell to the ground.

He covered his eyes
and was ripped
from his seat,
broke into a thousand pieces.

Whisper, My Everything

I got off the train
and walked into traffic.

The sea of engines parted,
whispers
of all around me.

Every step
moved by desire:
to get across,
to get to the other side.

Then everything,
all at once,
honking,
the woman rushing,
holding her dog to her chest,
bumping into the man
in front of her,
the truths,
gliding into one another,
so free of
and full of promise.

Sticky Eyelids

Before the caffeine kick start,
the wash basket
is filled with clothes
drenched in sweat.

I brush my teeth,
watch my gums bleed
in the mirror.

I wet my hair,
run my fingers through with
another layer of artificial grease.

Be presentable,
I think.

I splash aftershave
over stubbles and spots
and here I go,

kissing the day.

The Misfortune of Forgetfulness

Everyone wants something:
an apology,
an acknowledgement,
forgiveness.

Don't want something.

Don't ask for hand-outs,
or give them to those now in need
to create resentment.

Don't think of the past:
relationships building
an entwined future.

Let's find that place again
we lost a while back.

Together We'll Smile

Don't listen too close.

I don't want you to hear
how they talk about you,
mock your dreams.

Just come with me.

Together we'll smile.

Hand-in-hand,
we'll lead the way.

Daydream comes,
a songbird hums,
it flies away.

Eyes closed.

One day,
we'll remember that place
were the sun
never goes down.

The Journeyman Found His Way Home

I reflect
on the mediocrity
of the present.

Tired.

Sore from opportunity gone by,
my knife slides through
the half-cooked
bloodied meat.

I pray before bed
and ask to be taken back
to that world beneath my sheets.

Nothing happens.

My chair
at the centre of the room
is a glacier at sea.

Music on Public Transport

All of the best songs are slow.

Headphones keep life
at a distance.

Songs repeat,
create a beat
that no one hears.

The anti-social generation
listens without courtesy,
tinny sounds
come out
of their bent plastic.

Life's Running Track

She's been left behind
and imagines
footsteps behind her:
a party in her honour.

She wants a life
justified by what she owns,
not what she's lost.

And the crowd at her funeral
weep at the loss
of someone who never
saw the world.

Whiskey Induced Giggles in Greenland

You could spot her
in the frozen tundra.

Her eyes grey-pale
as she hid under each snowflake
falling, drifting
in the wind.

Her cheeks were raw,
tense beneath a pressure
she was unable to halt.

In the shelter of love
she shook each new flake
just for her.

And we talked
under the starlight,
just enough alcohol
to keep us warm.

My Friends at the East India

We share curry,
shroud ourselves in talk
old and new.

It's our past we enter,
no one but us
was there.

And we messed it up
behind closed doors,
our mistakes,
hidden in the dark.

We fell,
each other's spirits
shaped in the shape of love.

Now, over this curry,
our forks swirl around
and meet at the bottom,
push apart.

Nihilist Cat

Resting after her killing spree,
brown canned food
greets her nihilistic purr.

Denying the past,
of unwanted, undead,
bloodied gifts at the doorstep
of the strictest mistress,
she dives into dinner,
then struts to the litter tray.

Dissatisfied,
she wretches,
but with wings clipped,
she settles
to contentment.

The Bear Dances with a Red-Headed Girl on Snow

His paw held her hand
and the world looked on.

Their feet became numb in the snow
and sweat glistened on their brows.

Beyond the slavering jowls
she had to feel her part,
forsake hope of
what people perceived.

She fell in love with the stars
and the bear,
both whirled around her.

I Want to Be With the River

I want to live
where you live.

But I can't reach
the low lying rocks.

We cry,
me in the raft,
you bubbling,
at the bottom.

Desecrate the ground
when you overflow.

The Echo of the Chair

Backrest crashes
and legs splinter
on terracotta.

You:
swing left to right,
wriggle in desperation,
just above the floor.

You depart.

Me:
reach for a knife
to cut through the rope,
get you out.

I weep.

Then watch life rush back.

Through your bloodied nostrils
your breath breaks free.

Light bursts from your eyes.

Gather and Collect What's Been Discarded

The vile words
that haemorrhaged you
will be dumped
under the dark skies.

You'll be able to live again:
drink and dance,
kiss and talk
while the monsters
under your bed
watch you with envy,
because you no longer
need them
to watch you scrape by.

IV

National Borders

Arrogant men,
Who've forgotten what they'd do
if they had to look
into the eyes
of starving,
gaunt,
torn faces
of displaced children,
fight
for borders.

Armed,
with privilege
of birth,
skin pale,
they build.

Restricting entry
into
god given lands
they swore to protect
from ailing masses
looking for sanctuary.
No wise man
stops a family growing,
by starving the provider
of the tools of their enterprise,

and punishes
them for being "foreign" born.

We all came
from one place.
We were,
all the same.
Still are.
But in your rush to
secure superiority
you've forgotten that
want is not need.

You Marked Me

You marked me
with kisses.

So where did you expect me to go?
Rejected by my tribe,
your history,
our relationship,
my curse as I carry your sign
while you skin care, tender, clean.

Down the path
you lied for us,
as we danced
and pranced
through the starlight
of our youthful days of
exuberance?

Skip to the present
and you see you left me
behind.

In anticipation
of a change of heart,
and lust fuelled redemption,
I prayed
that you would take

me
and praise
me
and love
me
as yours.
If I walk back
down your pathway
and press my scarred flesh into your purity
will you hold out
and resist temptation
of others
and make me yours?

Secrets and Pound Coins

I'm sad
because I can't make
You care
about the basic injustice
at Your door.
Feed the children,
clothe the poor,
heal the sick.
Not a million miles away
from the ideals
of which
Your god spoke.

Why do You
work to fund
silent millionaires
but begrudge a starving child,
in
Your town,
on
Your street
a meal? Once a day. Five out of seven days a week.

Why should a child
go to bed
belly aching,
head throbbing

with hunger
and angst?
Why can't We provide?
Why won't You provide?

Bonfire Night Beneath the Stars

Penny for the guy,
and the girl,
in the sleeping bag
on the doorstep
of a shop that made
£67.4 million profit,
after avoiding tax,
in the financial year
2012-13,
ensuring the closure
of libraries, hostels, and A&E units,
in the financial year
2013-14.

Hold the shivering to account,
as fireworks illuminate
their faces distressed,
torn, worn with memories of misfortune.
Self-made in your eyes.
Approach your temple,
walk on proud,
and make sure
you don't remember their face,
as you step over them,
to offer praise
and thanks for your blessings.

Forget that times have fallen
harder on them,
than the discomfort you feel,
walking past to preach and pray
and hear from God's messenger
peace and justice for all.

Because We Must

My friend the defender
stood her ground,
then took theirs.

Decapitating words
uttered by bullies
who spit adjective bullets
at a silent
gracious scared youth.

To all that face
a hand serving
ill meaning,
we're with you,
because we must.

You that scream at us,
bile fuelled,
we know really you're hurting
as much as us.

Know that
if you take a public platform
to humiliate and defame,
you'll be beaten back
by sense,
bravery,
and common decency.

All the Kisses

I knew if you kissed him
he'd still walk away,
he'd already chosen.
I knew
that by the time he arrived
you'd be gone,
gone for him,
over there,
somewhere.
I knew when you ordered a drink,
you'd wait and contemplate
what would happen,
if he never turned up.
I knew he'd already found
someone he'd wanted.
So you waited in vain.
So he chased in vain.
And I knew that when you kissed him
he didn't kiss you back.
And so we waited,
holding the drink,
me in place of him.

No More Favours

Ask a favour
bend the ear
of those near.
Hark,
good advice
fresh,
individualised
to your need,
ready to be consumed
only by you.
But you push back
telling them
that they just don't
understand,
and they turn away.
Perceived chaos
of the day
too loud
to listen over
blocking what they say.
You let them walk,
still ignorant,
like the rest.

Window

Still photographs.
Sound crackling
from the gramophone in the attic
but you remain gone,
over exposed
in shaky camera shots
of the star,
taken from a balcony
two hundred feet away.

You missed the moment,
forgot to live.

Gone are the footprints of owls
in clay
that were their mark
long after
their last flight.

I implored you to
throw back your net curtains,
only used for twitching,
to blow the dust that seals your windowsill,
fling out the glass in wooden frame
and breathe.

But you knew best,
you missed it all,
in the pursuit of nature
via your search engine.

Old Age

Subversive chronicles
of corruption
by our great protectors
are doing the rounds,
surprising no one.

Waking minds,
stirred only by the fact
that action should have been taken
when it was rumour.
Uncomfortable with facing
a truth, the lies,
of their leaders,
only tentative steps of protest
were made by some,
mocked by the others,
the ones things hurt most.

You can prop up a generation,
who saw their parents
trodden into the dirt,
children who saw depression
and the degradation
of those who have them life
and yet,
for all the screams and shouts
they just laugh and drink

and say *that's the way things are.*

You can't make them stand.

Last Tube Home

The last tube,
from Kennington
to High Barnet,
cleanses me
from the misconception that
I am unequal
to the challenge of today.
Ear scratching patrons,
of the last train north,
show me their
yellow sticky filth
as they squelch their fingers
from tight lobe,
to public eye.
Some get on,
and off a stop later,
one happened to be an ex,
the rest strangers,
and then into the night,
they leave you alone to hope
of the best
for the rest,
of your night.

Tube Flames

Speaking with a sneer,
so you can hear,
I'm the voice of the underground,
bringing hellfire down
on your Dre beats.
I stamp my feet
and curl my arms,
blood pounding through
taut veins
eager to condemn
your social ignorance.
Blissful you are
behind *dum fun dum fun*
making sure we're all aware
of your song.

Political Appointment

I am a political appointment,
one forged in the blast furnace
of your ideology.
We are the slag your actions leave behind,
as you continue to douse the spirit
of my neighbours
less lucky than I,
who claimed from the state,
whose lives are a state
confined to a chair,
from where they bare their soul
once a fortnight
to a bureaucrat behind a desk
instructed to condemn them.

I am a political appointment,
not a flag waving
rosette wearer,
but one forced by you
to take a stand
and defend our land
so that those who live,
and those that come,
can find relief for the ailments
that steal away their night's rest.

I am a political appointment
who kneels
and calls for their mother,
face taut,
footprints scaring my clothes
as you repel my right to stand,
as I am doing nothing more than holding a placard
displaying my belief that,
in my most humble manner,
you're wrong.

I am a political appointment,
and you're unkind,
but leading our land.

Ode to the Silent Residents of Tower Blocks

Lowder House speaks volumes
about how we treat our kin.
Tucked between the restored factory walls of the Tobacco
Dock
and the city moulding Thames,
a stone's throw from where Murdoch's bile mongers
churned hell on poor quality paper and badly set
newsprint that sticks to the fingers and
the graves of the careers of journalists and print workers
who, revelling in the tears of the trade unionists who wept
for the families, are hungry and facing the unknown.

Poverty wrapped in the stale concrete wrapper of grey
concrete, brown fascias,
metal grates covering the windows and doors of the
lowest set flats.
No one ever knocks on the doors of Lowder House
to listen to tales of unemployment struggles
and children in hand-me-downs
kicking a burst football between bricks,
using the discarded cans of drunks as goalposts.

Even if they did though,
their attempts at conversation would be stunted by
modest refusals from people who just,
well, they can't trust those who have, time and time,
ignored their needs
without even a passing smile.

They don't plead,
they scream,
but their tormented retching has been ringing off the
walls of the city for so long
that we're deaf to them.

In our faces their tonsils vibrate
but their image dissipates
from our consciousness
because their head scarf, or skin tone, or the smell of
their cuisine
helps them to camouflage into something that we can't
quite take seriously enough to see.

With all the world's media in their sights,
for so many decades,
the quietest voice
seeps out of Lowder House
and we'll never remember our neighbours.

Idealism

Tell me,
oh, sorry to disturb you but I must ask:
you
sat their watching the wide screen
on tick from the catalogue
microwaving your dinner,
why have you let someone born into money
tell you that equality and fairness is idealism and cannot,
no,
should not happen?

When a man stands up for the jobs of the men and
women who face seeing their families go without unless
he does,
you scoff
and ridicule
and make snide comments to television cameras shoved
in your face
to gage your reaction at having to walk a mile to work.

When a man stands alone on a podium
below the banner of those disposed before
as a reminder that it can happen to anyone,
and he tells you that you deserve better,
you jeer
and turn away.

You read your history books in school,
and saw the women chained to the railings,
being beaten, arrested, then force fed,
but on polling day you stay at home
then complain that your means of survival are cut,
your prescriptions cost more
and your child has more homework in a night than you
had in a month.

You dare to complain,
when it's not fair on
you.

You
dare to say your tax pounds shouldn't help those who
have fallen on hard times
while expecting support yourself,
because in your case—
it's not your fault.

Despite this,
you buy your Christmas presents online,
your coffee in chains,
and your phone contract from people who don't con-
tribute a penny to your National Health Service.

The teachers, tube drivers, and firemen who stand to-
gether
for their right to have a career with the remuneration
they went into it being promised,

or worse,
standing together for their jobs,
are openly mocked and humiliated in the press,
and the streets.

Why have you let people tell you that the basic rights of
others are wrong?

Wake up and realise that idealism isn't wrong,
idealism can happen—
if only you made the decision to make it happen.

The Last Work House in London

In the dawn shadow,
cast by the last workhouse in London,
a street sweeper brushes the cigarette butts
and chicken bones that seep out of bright red boxes
past a sleeping bag
and into her garbage chariot.

Slumped against a wheelie bin,
like the other bags of discard from the city,
the sleeping bag emits a faint snore that creeps into the
first light,
making sure commuters know to tread softly.

She catches her brush on the sleeping bag, the street
sweeper does.
Every morning she knocked it as she passed,
to stir it before the road was too populous and it drowns
in the tide of travel.

The sleeping bag,
before each high rise dawn,
births a man who sits
upright, building up a smile to greet the day
as big as the towers in sight of his bed.
His belly rumbling with such a magnitude
that it can have been mistaken for the tube train
rattling the tracks below.

Roused,
he stands,
pulling the sleeping bag down to reveal a plaid shirt,
green khakis with a black belt in survival holding them
up,
and maroon trainers,
once victorious in the race for the last bus home—a
time forgot.

His newspaper pillow,
damp with sweat and dew,
he folds
and puts inside his sleeping bag
alongside his torn bed sheet that helped to kept the
worst of the insects off.

This good find outside a charity shop door
drapes him as he rises
and lies down at night,
like a Lord Mayor awaiting entrance to a royal feast.

Packed up,
he strides towards the towers of the city,
a nod to the street cleaner as she works her way toward
the high street.

King of it all, in his sheet. His dignity preserved by his
black belt in survival.

Loving You

Tonight was,
it was the last time I'll ever see you,
and I didn't even think to kiss you goodnight.

Tip tap, tip tap.
Your fingers
in time to the music,
like Morse code
pleading with me to rescue you from
the monotony of tonic after gin
and another empty glass slamming on the table.
With your handbag over your shoulder,
a little red thing too small for anything but your keys,
you swayed
your smile waning with the tune.

As you broke away from your friends,
you headed my way.
My brow flooded with lifeless drunken sweat
and my palms the same.
My leg shook,
but my free hand held it still
as your hair whipped the air closer to me
and refreshed my flushed red nose with a perfumed
breeze.
When you were level with me,
at the edge of the varnished dance floor,

I leant toward you—
just to say hello.
My toe caught on the sticky club carpet
and I lurched forward,
my forehead intercepting the journey of your face to its
destination,
and my glass slid melancholy to the floor
in the moment of silence that followed,
smashing on impact and making sensual looking stains
across the front of my trousers.

Blood splattered,
you looked like a fallen angel,
fallen from the top of a tall building and landing to
grace me.
But as the tears began to swell
it seemed apparent that you'd not be going home with
me,
accidents happen,
I just wish I'd worn my Converse,
their soles barely grip.

Tonight was, it was the first time I ever saw you,
and I didn't even think
to ask your name.

Empty Carriage

There was just my bag
on the empty tube train.
It wasn't rush hour,
but it was eerie
like the morning after the bombings
that shattered the city.
That day,
like this,
I was a line ranger
facing the solitude of the underground
in my lengthy stride.
In a place where you do not speak to strangers,
I feel lost without them by my side.
As I travel up the tracks
in my steel white carriage,
with its blue and red insignia,
I'm relieved to be joined by evening merry drunks
and people on the post-theatre comedown
and some
just on their way home.
They all have a story of tonight,
of every night of every day they've enjoyed and endured.
But tonight is not the night for those.
Maybe one day
I'll share my story with my carriage fellows,
but until then I turn my music up,
put my head down,

and plough on home,
safe in the knowledge that I'm not alone.

Lightning Speed

Train pulls away
north bound.
More vivid with each mile,
memories of my childhood:
travelling with my dad
to football games
and drinking from a juice box
and tearing into a chocolate bar,
only remembering
to offer a bite
as I approach the end,
and we talked about
the prospect of victory.
Then a flurry
of activity,
pulling my rucksack from the luggage rack
and
with a whirr automatic doors,

I'm home.

Acknowledgements

Dominic wishes to acknowledge the editors and staff of the following magazines, anthologies, and journals who chose work from this collection for their pages:

City Lit Rag
Spontaneity Arts Journal
The Cadaverine
Poetry and Paint
Pankhearst/Starshy
United Press
Prole
Forward Poetry
Buzz Magazine

About the Author

Dominic Stevenson is an English-born writer with his roots in the post-industrial north of England. His aim is to take part in the global discussions surrounding societal, gender, sexual, and educational equality.

His first collection, *The Northern Line*, was released in March, 2015. His poetry and short stories have been published in a range of print and online publications including *Litro Magazine*, *City Lit Rag*, *Forward Poetry*, *The Cadaverine*, and *Spontaneity Arts Journal*.

Follow Dom:
fantasticaldom.com
Twitter: @Fantastical_Dom
Facebook: facebook.com/fantasticaldom

www.ingramcontent.com/pod-product-compliance
Lightning Source LLC
Chambersburg PA
CBHW070813050426
42452CB00011B/2030